# One Oddity's Odyssey

Samiat Quadir

BookLeaf Publishing

India | USA | UK

Presentation by *BookLeaf Publishing*

Web: www.bookleafpub.com

E-mail: info@bookleafpub.com

ISBN: 9789358311853

First edition 2023

# ACKNOWLEDGEMENT

I would like to thank my sister, who kept believing in me when I didn't. Thank you for being annoying and pushing me to do this. You are the best!

# Beyond the Sea: A Classic

Somewhere beyond the sea,
Is a perfect me, who can do anything.
A me, who lives so wild and free,
Relinquished from pressures that wrap like a coil
spring.

An unchained melody, unbound from my
shackles,
Untethered, I flow whichever way the wind
dictates.
A fluid motion, there is nothing I can't tackle.
Too much to explore, no time to fixate.

Don't let me be misunderstood.
I am not free, or a perfect me, you see.
Not yet at least, I hope someday I could,
All I have to do is go somewhere beyond the
sea.

# The Shore

I stand on the bed of the shore and stare
outward,
Paralyzed by forces beyond my control
I feel myself on the edge of the precipice
looking beyond the horizon,
A vast, limitless ocean ahead of me, and an
endless chasm beneath.

Tales of eons past sing songs of heroes
Who dared to pierce the veil of the comfort of
stasis.
They didn't have time to stare into the abyss,
Instead their eyes remain fixated on the path
beyond.

I'm no hero. I am transfixed as the sands of time
dwindle,
Too afraid to leave the shore, too ashamed to
head back.
Heroes aren't scared of the unknown, I am
petrified,
A statue locked in place by a cruel sculptor. I am
no Odysseus.

# No Odysseus

What is a hero? I find myself asking this
question,
Day by day, with no answer to cure the plague in
my mind.
Does a hero face the beast with bravery and
courage?
I do not know, for I am no hero. I am no
Odysseus.

The Journey beyond wicks away at any bravado,
The courage that was once strong, dissipating as
a drop of water.
Does a hero face forward, with conviction true
as his heart?
I do not know, for I am no hero. I am no
Odysseus.

The waves wash away any certainty for the path
beyond,
Leaving me with only a cloud of doubt, a storm
raging inward.
Does a hero compose lyrics of inspiration,
leading his people forward?
I do not know, for I am no hero. I am no
Odysseus.

The hopeful glance of the grew dimming as the
day carries on,
Their numbers dwindling like the autumn leaves
of a branch.
A hero can be many things, courageous, true,
and inspirational.
I am not any of these things. But I can be.

I can be all these things and more.
Just like how spring chases after winter, with
flowers blossoming
On once dead trees, I can shed a new skin and
become anew.
I am no hero, but I will be.

# Haiku #1: Adventures Await

Adventures Await,
Excited beyond belief,
Hopefully Optimistic.

# Ode To Sea

I see nothing but clear skies ahead
A blank canvas, I can paint the skies how I see
fit.

The gentle wind embraces me softly as the sun
warms my soul.
I feel free and limitless, as the sounds of the
ocean cheer me on.

Go on! Go on! I am buoyed by my hopes and
dreams.
Kept afloat by my ship, edging ever closer to my
destiny.

Even Posiedon is on my side, as an ode to sea is
an ode to he.
He who is the God of the ocean, as I am the god
of me.

But this is an Ode to sea. A love story to the
oceans that brings life.
That gives a sense of wonder for all to see.

# A Calm: The Impending Storm

A blanket of stillness covers the ocean ground,
As a false sense of security lulls us towards
The sound of silence - so loud, wrapping us all
around,
Coveting the noise of the floorboards.

There's a pause of tranquility, breathing in
The blurred moment where life stood still.
Moonlight caresses the unmoving waters even in
Darkness, shimmering bright as the tears that
could spill.

No waves, or rushing wind to push us forward,
The silence begins to water the seed of doubt
As worry creeps up with the ocean's wayward
Tendencies to lash and act out.

She's a fickle mistress, brewing a storm in the
distance,
Not one you can see, but feel in the still air.
With nowhere to go, and no resistance,
The rush of storms we must soon bear.

# In The Distance: The Storm Approaches

In the distance, I see a storm
Dark, as clouds gather and hide the sun.
The waves come crashing, rocking the vessel,
As the rain dances on the ocean floor.

In the distance, I hear a storm,
As thunder serenades lightning,
Singing symphonies and whispering sweet
nothings,
Of a marriage to be bound together.

In the distance, I feel the storm,
Now, no longer so far, inching ever closer,
As the pelts of rain bombard the ship,
Signaling that the storm is here.

# Roaring in: The Raging Storm

A storm always comes roaring in,
The rush of sounds reverberates through my bones,
Thunder echoes in the distance as rain starts pouring in,
More within, my heart's racing and muscles are stones.

More like hundreds of tiny pebbles stitched together,
Forever, by a singular string that stretches thin.
A precious thing, not strong enough for this weather,
Whether I could sustain or not, maybe answered herein.

I have to avoid the storm in some way,
Somehow, I must deny its very existence.
Resistance may be futile someday.
The storm always comes but I must maintain persistence.

# The Cyclops: Eye of the storm

Within mere moments, the roaring winds calm,
As tranquility envelopes the ship, masking us
From the dangers of the harsh storm.
The eye of the storm watches us, like a Cyclops,
Holding a strength with a calm gaze. I am
nobody.
In the eye of the storm we find peace.
Her gaze, ever so captivating, brings the light
that kisses our skin
Allures us, and gives us a false promise of hope,
As we steal a moment's peace, recapturing our
breaths.
Her gentle winds whisper of a tale too fresh,
Nearing ever closer, only a blink away.
We embrace the stillness, recouping from the
damage,
As we know that in this eye, she is heeding her
warning,
That only beyond the calm is another tempest
brewing.

# Ride The Wave: Enduring The Storm

The waves come crashing against my vessel,
knocking me around.
I can't seem to get a grip, everything seems like
it's slipping away.
The offbeat rhythm of the waves, ringing
disorientating sounds.
It echos violently within me, as my body begins
to sway.

Back and forth I go, and side to side I slide.
My bearings begin to dissipate, as the thin line
between fear and hope begins to fade.
Waves of emotion hit me as tides,and there is no
place to hide.
I can't turn back now, hopeless now, I must still
ride the wave.


I must endure the storm.

# Haiku #2: After The Storm

I am lost at sea,
Floating endlessly forever,
Wanting salvation.

# The Siren

Her voice, a gentle whisper in the ocean,
Like a drop of water in the vast desert sand.
The melody, so sweet, luring forth bittersweet
emotion,
The emotion and desperation for her promise of
land.

She called out my name, with the taste of home
on her lips,
Her tendrils coil, enticing, sly and sly,
A whispered lure, igniting the flame within the
ships
A dance of darkness, where the men will die.

In her grasp, my soul begins to fray,
Her gaze, like a forbidden fruit, tantalizing in its
taste,
But in my resistance, her hold begins to sway,
My inner battle, demanding to leave with haste.

Hide away, and block the sound from your ears
As her screech holds with a tight grip true like
iron,
Her beauty fades, replaced with something made
from your fears,

For beneath the surface, was a creature known as The Siren.

# Enchantment: Calypso

Tempted by the sins of life, and the pleasures of
lust
Where wild dreams come true, I dare not
discuss.
Resolute, I remain, but I am on the cusp
Of realizing a fantasy, and attain it I must.

In doing so, I'll lose myself, then who will I
trust?
The Siren beckons me as my head lay on her
bust.
Visions fill my head of delight from Dawn till
dusk.
Calypso promises me I will never turn to dust.

She promises to vanquish death as my foe, I just
Can't shake the feeling I'm needed somewhere. I
must
Journey back home, I will need to adjust.
Traverse back the path I once traveled and be
robust.

She has me in her clutches; from mistress so
unjust.

Tied to her whims, I swim in her pools till my
heart begins to rust.
She becomes explosive and I escape while she
combusts.
Like a thief in the night, I steal my freedom and
move in forward thrust.

I must return home at once.

# The Lotus Eaters

I embark on this land unknown,
Never touched by the legends before.
This land that I can call on my own,
With mysterious whispers filling the shore.

From the trees, come friendly strangers,
With gifts and fruits for all to eat.
The juices spill, washing away the dangers,
Instead increasing the thirst for this treat.

A kaleidoscope of hues, the sun sets on the
crystal waters,
The light fading with our memories, so distant
and far away
And desires to return back to our sons and
daughters,
Dissipate, left with the hunger for home that's
kept at bay.

Alarms blast, a frantic warning echoing in my
ear,
Nulling the taste of nature, that's causing such
ail.
With the past returning, my men I must steer,
And leave this island by setting sail.

# Haiku #3: Journey Back

18

I follow the stars,
As they lead me back to home.
I must maintain course.

# Haiku #4: Where I belong

I am comfortable,
Knowing what I overcame,
No longer afraid.

# The Shore (Reprise):

I am no Odysseus. No sculptor would make a
statue of me.
Petrified no longer I now look for the unknown,
Ready to head back, eager to leave the shore.
Time stands still for no one, not even the hero.

My eyes are engrossed by the path of return.
I stared into the abyss, and it stared back as a
reflection of myself.
The static look of comfort shrouds my destiny.
The heroes ambition tells tales of future songs
yet to be unsung

I walk atop of an infinite chasm, with an
expansive, boundless ocean behind,
Feeling as if I have dived off the precipice and
into the horizon.
Now I am in control, and able to maneuver as I
please
I lay on the bed of the shore, and stare inward.

# Reflection

The sands beneath my feet feel warm to touch,
The grain slipping through my palms,
As if they, too, mourn the loss of this journey.
I am alone now, with no one to share
The long lost feeling of home,
Only a breath away,
Past the ocean of sand,
Beneath the warm summer skies.
I missed home, no more than I miss my crew.
But some things, I can't get back,
No matter how hard I try
So I must move forward,
With only a reflection of my past self,
So eager and innocent, unwilling to learn what
loss means.
I am smarter now, more powerful,
As the ocean has taught me, that we do not need
to be heroes,
Lost in the ocean, with only our tales to continue
our legacy.
Even Odysseus came back home, with nothing
but time,
To ever indicate that he left.
I must do the same, and walk forward
Ever closer to the lost promise of my bed.

My home.
My life.

# There's No Place Like Home

My heart yearns for the familiar scent of home,
And with renewed memories, I set my feet
homeward,
And commence a new journey where I roam
For only a moment until I walk forward.

It's been so long, since I've seen this familiar
sky,
The clouds joyous for my return,
As I am greeted as an ally,
No - a hero, who went through so much to learn.

The walls of home embraced my tight,
Beckoning me to find my bed and lay down,
And get a moment's rest and forget the fight.
As I slept, I felt glad to be back in town.

# Haiku #5: Eternal Slumber



I have returned home.
My soft, motionless bed waits.
I slumber with peace.